Calling all aliens!

Are you planning a holiday to planet Earth?

Finn and Zeek are here to help.

'Super Bees'
Published by MAVERICK ARTS PUBLISHING LTD

Studio 11, City Business Centre, 6 Brighton Road,
Horsham, West Sussex, RH13 5BB, +44 (0)1403 256941
© Maverick Arts Publishing Limited February 2020

A CIP catalogue record for this book is available at the British Library.

ISBN 978-1-84886-676-8

www.maverickbooks.co.uk

Credits:
Finn & Zeek illustrations by Jake McDonald, Bright Illustration Agency
Cover: Jake McDonald/Bright, ©Konrad Wothe/Minden / naturepl.com
Inside: **Naturepl.com:** ©Heather Angel (6-7), ©Clay Bolt (9), ©Eric Baccega (10),
©Mark Taylor (11, 21, 24), ©MD Kern / Palo Alto JR Museum (12), ©Stephen Dalton
(12), ©Kim Taylor (13), ©Laurent Geslin (13), ©Eric Baccega (14-15, 27), ©Gary K. Smith
(15, 28), ©Konrad Wothe/Minden (16), ©Phil Savoie (18-19), ©Pal Hermansen (20),
©Cheryl-Samantha Owen (22), ©Mark Moffett (23), ©Gavin Hellier (23), ©Nick Upton
(24), ©Will Watson (25), ©Stephen Dalton (25),

Gold

This book is rated as: Gold Band (Guided Reading)

Super Bees

Contents

INCOMING MESSAGE

Dear Finn and Zeek

We want to visit Earth, and we're hoping to see some bees. Please can you tell us why these insects are so important to humans, animals and the planet?

Yours,
Flo and Hon
(Planet Drone)

Introduction

Bees are flying insects that live all over the world. They might be small, but they have superpowers that make them very important.

Bees **pollinate** plants, and this helps the plants to make seeds. Then new plants grow from the seeds. If this didn't happen, life on Earth would be in serious trouble. Plants provide homes for wildlife, food for humans and animals, and even the air that people breathe.

Bees aren't just brilliant at pollination – they also make honey, a yummy sweet food that humans love to eat.

If you scare a bee, it might sting you.

Across the world, there are as many as 20,000 **species** of bee. In the UK alone, there are more than 250 species!

All bees have six legs, wings, a hard outer shell called an exoskeleton, a pair of **antennae** and three main body parts: head, thorax and abdomen.

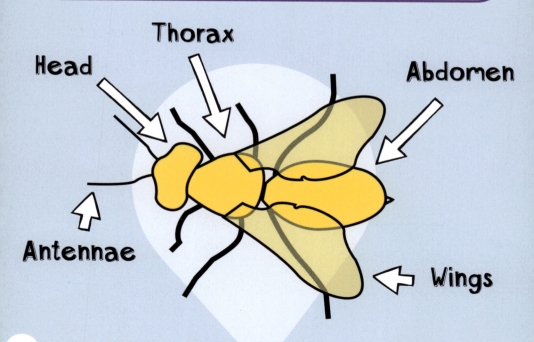

Head

Thorax

Abdomen

Antennae

Wings

Bees come in many different sizes. One of the smallest is the North American Perdita minima which is less than 2mm long. The largest is thought to be the Megachile pluto from Indonesia which can grow to almost 4cm.

Honey bee

Megachile pluto

A Megachile pluto looks huge compared to a honey bee!

Not all bees are yellow and black. Some are orange, green, blue and even purple!

Bees can sting, but only if they get surprised or scared. The sting feels like a sharp pinch and will turn into a little red lump. This can be painful and itchy but it will get better by itself.

People who work with bees are called beekeepers. Beekeepers wear special clothing for protection.

Some people are allergic to bee stings, which means they can get ill if they are stung. They need to take medicine as soon as they've been stung.

When young humans are stung they need to tell a grown-up straight away!

11

One of the most famous bee species on Earth is the European honey bee. As well as honey, it also makes beeswax. Beeswax can be used for candles, wood polish and even face cream!

Follow the life cycle of a honey bee...

2 After three days, the egg hatches into a **larva**.

1 A tiny egg is laid inside the beehive by the **queen bee**.

3 The larva grows quickly, eating up to 1300 meals a day!

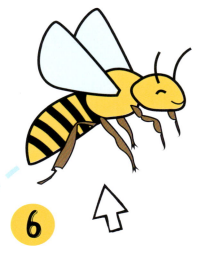

4 The larva spins a cocoon around its body and becomes a **pupa**.

6 After 21 days, this amazing insect is now ready to start life as an adult bee!

5 Over the next 12 days it develops eyes, legs, wings and fuzzy hair.

Honey is made by a **colony** of honey bees all working together in a big, buzzy team. There are between 10,000 to 60,000 bees in a typical beehive. First, worker bees fly out to collect **nectar** from flowers. When honey bees find a good place to get nectar, they let each other know by doing a little dance! They then take the nectar back to the hive.

The bees pass on the nectar to the bees at the hive, who chew it for half an hour to make it less runny. Bees also fan their wings over the nectar to help this! The nectar turns into honey, and the bees store it in a waxy **honeycomb**. They use it as food during the winter.

Humans can use the honey too, but beekeepers must be careful to leave enough for the bees.

Honey bees travel up to 55,000 miles to produce about one jar of honey!

What is Pollination?

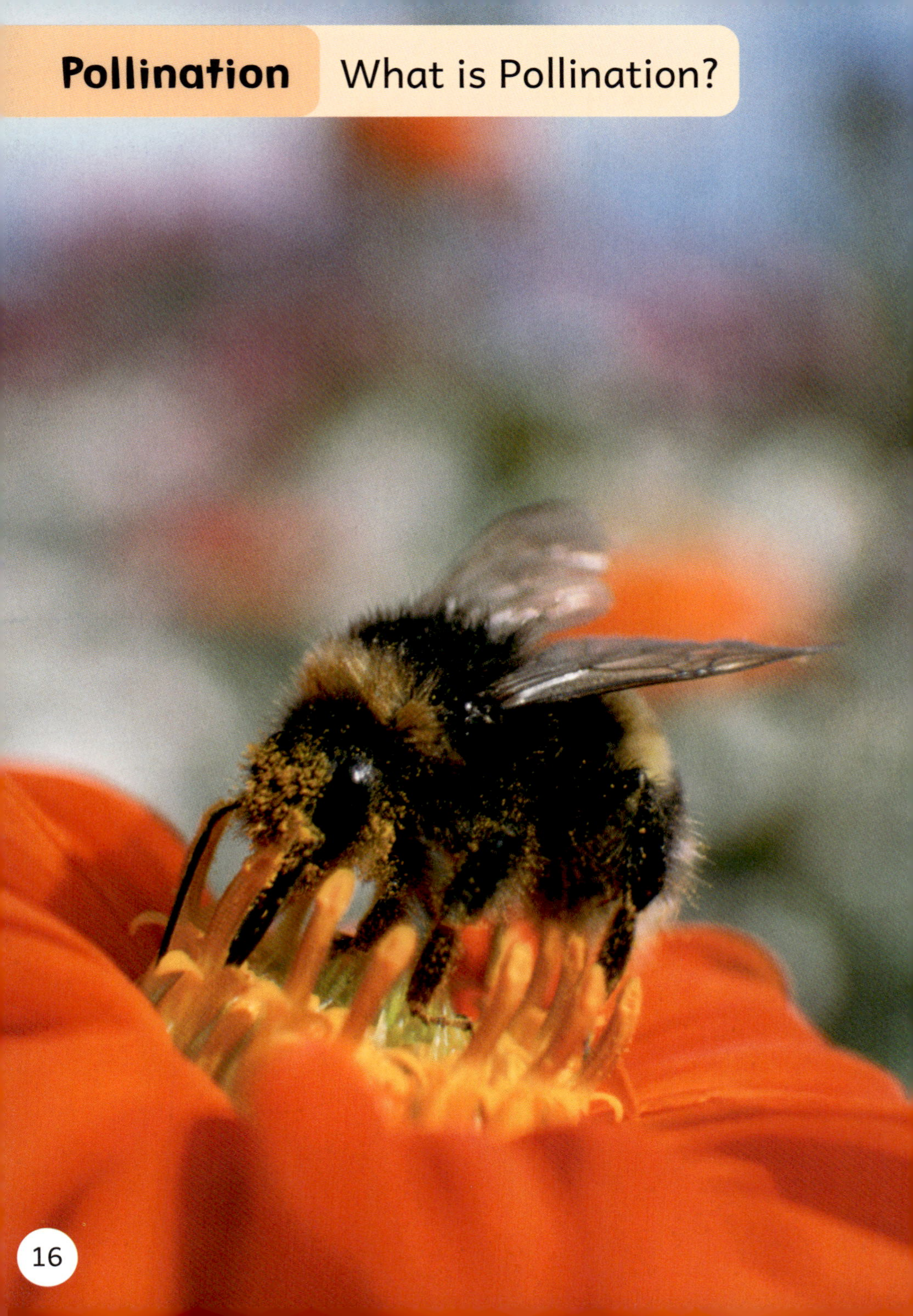

Pollen is a special powder found in flowers. In order for plants to make seeds, the pollen has to travel from one flower to another. Then seeds can start to grow.

The problem is that plants can't move by themselves! So bees help them by taking the pollen from one flower to another.

This powdery stuff is pollen!

Pollen also travels on the wind, and with the help of other insects, birds or bats.

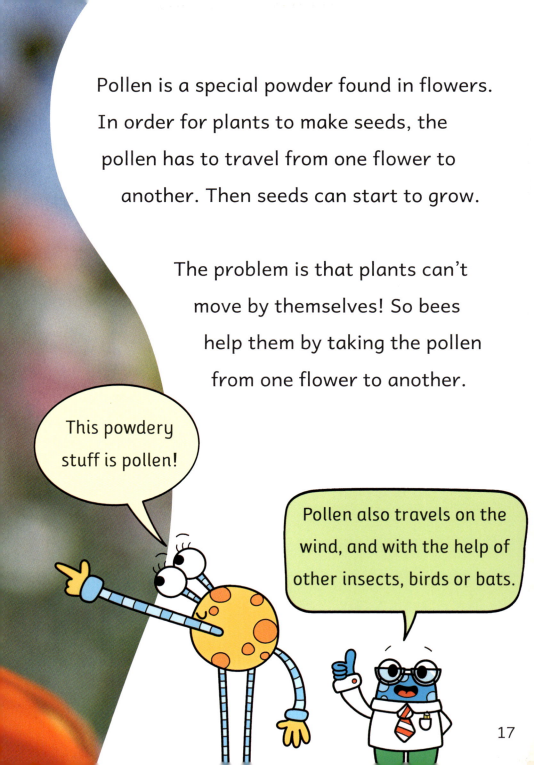

Follow Bella Bee as she pollinates a flower.

1 ⇨

Bella spots a colourful flower and zooms into action. She lands on the flower to feed on its delicious nectar.

As she's feeding, pollen from the flower sticks to her fuzzy body.

⇦ **2**

3

Bella flies onto a neighbouring flower – she is hungry for more nectar. The pollen she collected rubs off onto the new flower.

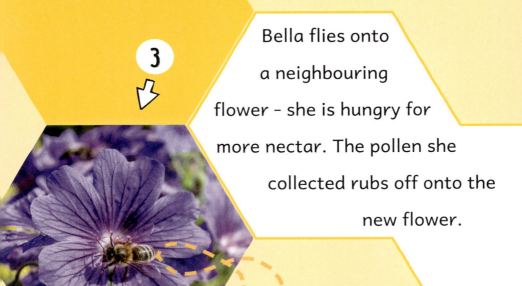

Hooray! Now seeds can start to grow inside the flower. Lots of new plants will grow from the seeds.

4

Without pollination by bees and other insects, many plants could not survive. Farmers would struggle to grow vegetables and fruit.

With fewer plants around, lots of important **habitats** like wildflower meadows and orchards would be destroyed.

The result? Humans and other Earth animals could be left without food or shelter.

Some young humans might like the idea of a world without broccoli. But vegetables are important for a healthy diet!

Deadly Threat

All over Earth, pollinators are in peril. Some bee species have even become extinct. There are three main threats to Earth's bee superheroes...

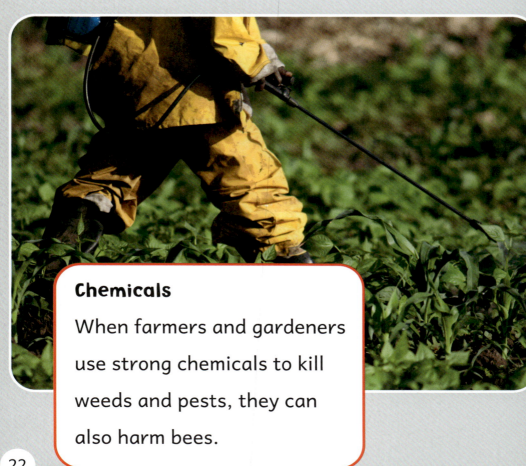

Chemicals

When farmers and gardeners use strong chemicals to kill weeds and pests, they can also harm bees.

Disease

Honey bees are under attack from a tiny bug called the Varroa mite. The bug makes the bees feel ill and weak.

Varroa mite

Habitat loss

As humans use up more and more of the land, bees lose the meadows, hedgerows and wild areas where they find flowers and food.

Saving the Superheroes

Humans are working hard to save Earth's precious bees. Everyone can help!

Here are some bee-friendly tips...

Grow different types of flowers, herbs, fruit trees and shrubs. Choose plants that flower at different times of the year, such as primroses in the spring, honeysuckle in the summer and sedum in the autumn.

Have an untidy patch in the corner of a garden to encourage wildlife and offer a shelter for bees.

Let grass grow longer and avoid using weedkiller on lawns. This will give daisies, clover, dandelions and buttercups a chance to flower – and local bees can enjoy a delicious picnic!

Bees need water as well as nectar. Put a shallow tray of fresh water in the garden so that bees can have a drink. Add in some stones or twigs to provide a landing platform!

Dear Flo and Hon,

Amazing eh? Bees are only small insects, but they play a MASSIVE part in keeping the Earth healthy.

We hope you're buzzing to visit Earth now. You might even get to taste some honey!

From,
Finn and Zeek x

A bee on a honeycomb

Look at the pollen on this bee's back legs!

1. What is the name for a group of bees?
a) Gang
b) Colony
c) Herd

2. What is the powdery stuff inside flowers called?
a) Pollen
b) Sherbet
c) Flour

3. What is a person who looks after bees called?

4. How can humans help bees?
a) By singing to them
b) By planting fruit trees
c) By building houses

5. What does an insect larva turn into?
a) A pooper
b) A pluto
c) A pupa

6. How many honey bees live in
a typical beehive?
a) 600
b) 20
c) Between 10,000 to 60,000

Turn over for answers

Index/Glossary

Antennae pg 8

Antennae are like extra-long noses for insects! They help bees to smell, taste and feel.

Colony pg 14

The name for a group of bees living together in a hive or nest.

Habitats pg 21, 23

The natural homes of animals, plants or other living things.

Honeycomb pg 15, 27

A group of small, waxy shapes, or 'cells', made by bees to store honey and eggs. Each cell is a hexagon (that's a shape with six sides).

Larva pg 12, 13

A baby insect that has left its egg but has not yet developed into a pupa or adult.

Nectar pg 14, 15, 18, 19

A sugary liquid made by plants.

Pollinate/pollination pg 6, 7, 16, 18, 20, 22

When bees fly from one flower to another, pollination takes place. Once a plant is pollinated, it can make seeds which will one day grow into new plants.

Pupa pg 13

The stage of an insect's life after it has become a larva and before it is an adult.

Queen bee pg 12

The queen bee is a large female bee that can lay eggs. There is only one queen bee in a hive.

Species pg 8, 12, 22

A group of living things that shares similarities. Different species of bee include the honey bee and bumblebee.

Book Bands for Guided Reading

The Institute of Education book banding system is a scale of colours that reflects the various levels of reading difficulty. The bands are assigned by taking into account the content, the language style, the layout and phonics. Word, phrase and sentence level work is also taken into consideration.

Maverick Early Readers are a bright, attractive range of books covering the pink to white bands. All of these books have been book banded for guided reading to the industry standard and edited by a leading educational consultant.

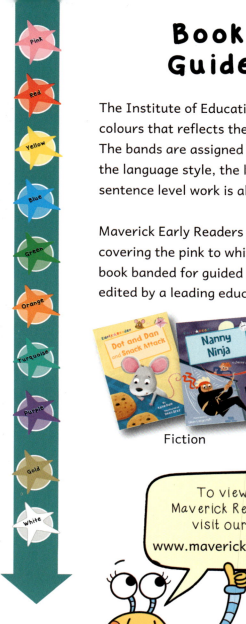

Fiction

Non-fiction

To view the whole Maverick Readers scheme, visit our website at
www.maverickearlyreaders.com

Or scan the QR code above to view our scheme instantly!